TRULY FREE
STUDY GUIDE

TRULY FREE

Breaking the Snares That So Easily Entangle

ROBERT MORRIS

With Kevin and Sherry Harney

W PUBLISHING GROUP

AN IMPRINT OF THOMAS NELSON

Published in Nashville, Tennessee, by W Publishing, an imprint of Thomas Nelson. W Publishing and Thomas Nelson are registered trademarks of HarperCollins Christian Publishing, Inc.

Published in association with the literary agency of Winters & King, Inc., an Author Management Company. www.wintersking.com.

Thomas Nelson titles may be purchased in bulk for educational, business, fundraising, or sales promotional use. For information, please e-mail SpecialMarkets@ ThomasNelson.com.

ISBN 978-0-7180-2857-2

First Printing May 2015 / Printed in the United States of America

CONTENTS

OF NOTE

The quotations interspersed throughout this study guide and the introductory comments are excerpts from the book *Truly Free* by Robert Morris and from the video curriculum of the same name. All other resources — including the session introductions, small group questions, and between-sessions materials — have been written by Kevin and Sherry Harney.

FREE AT LAST

Their desert grumblings started out something like this—
"What I wouldn't give right now to be back sitting in the shade of my old house in Egypt."

"Yeah," said another, a faraway look in her eyes. "We really had it good back there, didn't we?"

A third chimed in. "We sat around pots of meat and ate all the food we wanted. Remember all those fresh onions and garlic and leeks? So tasty!"

They felt the saliva in their mouths.

And from there the grumbling erupted.

Do you catch what important truth the Israelites had forgotten?

They'd been slaves!

The Israelites had escaped bondage in Egypt through the power of God, but in the wilderness they were still imprisoned by their mindsets and selective memory of life in Egypt.

Back in Egypt they might have eaten onions and garlic and leeks on rare occasions. But they also labored from dawn to dusk every day under the unbending order to make bricks without straw. Egypt came complete with cruel taskmasters and chains and shackles and poverty and whips. All their baby boys had once been thrown into the Nile River. Repeatedly—desperately—the Israelites had cried out to God for a deliverer.

Now they'd forgotten they had been in bondage!

And they'd forgotten God had answered their cry. God had sent a deliverer to lead them out of slavery.

But hold on a moment. Before we come down too hard on the Israelites, have you ever considered how susceptible we are today to do, or at least lean toward, the same thing?

If we're Christians, the Lord has delivered us from slavery. Through Christ's work on the cross, Jesus has removed our despair and darkness and put in its place victory, strength, and freedom. The old is gone. The new has come. We are a new creation (see 2 Corinthians 5:17). We never need to return to Egypt.

And yet ...

A life of slavery still beckons to us. We find our old, harmful thoughts are hard to shake. Our former unhealthy habits are hard to break. Long-embedded patterns of shameful living continue to entangle us, day after day, month after month, even year after year.

We need to recognize the reality and presence of the spiritual realm. We need to step fully into God's plan to heal our broken world. We need to move into life, healing, purity, liberty, holiness, and truth.

In the six sessions of this small group study, we will explore a glorious truth: *the promise of being set free from slavery is a promise to be set free completely.* Along the way, we'll surface a need you might not have even known you had. At this very moment, scriptural evidence exists that shows you can be negatively influenced by evil. That same evil can entrap you and harm you, oppress you and hurt you, and generally make your life difficult. It can even enslave you to harmful patterns of living.

But in this study we are not going to fixate on evil. I won't tell you prolonged stories of the bizarre, the cruel and unusual, or the weird. You won't hear stories that keep you awake at night. Instead, we will dwell on the *goodness, power, and truth of Jesus Christ.* We will focus on how *God sets us free.* All authority has been given to Jesus (see Matthew 28:18). He has conquered death, hell, and evil (see 1 Corinthians 15:54–56). He now reigns at God's right hand forevermore (see Acts 2:33).

The good news is, regardless of what difficulty you're struggling with today, there is always hope. Sure, the temptation never quite goes away in this life—the pull always exists toward becoming burdened again by a yoke of slavery (see Galatians 5:1). But you need to know—and live out fully—that you never need to return to Egypt.

With Jesus Christ, you can be truly free. I look forward to going on this journey with you.

—Robert Morris

Session One

GREATER IS HE

For we do not wrestle against flesh and blood, but ... against spiritual hosts of wickedness in the heavenly places.

EPHESIANS 6:12

Introduction

We live in a dangerous world. Just turn on the news, check the top stories online, or listen to people talking around the office or your neighborhood. The world is a perilous place and growing more so with each passing day. Going through an airport reminds us terrorism is real because everything is scanned, searched, and scrutinized. War rages around our planet, and reports are given twenty-four hours a day on cable news. Sickness and disease loom, financial crisis threatens, and political turmoil is ever present.

You might expect people to be paralyzed with fear and sobered by the reality of all the potential disaster surrounding them. But this does not seem to be the case. We have learned to adapt and press on. Consumers head to the mall and shop online with increasing optimism. Many people hop on planes with confident certainty everything will be fine. Viewers watch cooking shows, sitcoms, reality programs, and talent shows day after day as if everything is fine.

Let's be honest—pressing on and acting like things are okay are ways of coping. If we fixate on all the danger and trouble in the world, we will be consumed with it. We still need to sing, play, go to church, shop, raise families, and live our lives … even when the world is in turmoil. Part of survival involves not letting these realities dominate our lives or control our thinking.

But wait! When it comes to the spiritual battles and dangers around us, we can't take the same posture. If we ignore the spiritual attacks, landmines, and dangers around us, it will cost us more than we imagine.

We can't look the other way, become numb, or just move along with our lives. We must wake up, pay attention, and walk in the power of the Holy Spirit. If we look the other way, we will find ourselves in spiritual bondage. If we want to be truly free, we need to face the battle and resist the work of the devil in this world. To do this we must walk in the power of the One who is greater and infinitely more powerful than the enemy of our souls.

When we understand this, we are on the path to freedom.

If you are in bondage, you can get truly free!

Talk About It

Welcome to the first session of Truly Free: Breaking the Snares That So Easily Entangle. *If you or any of your fellow group members do not know one another, take some time to introduce yourselves. To get things started, discuss one of the following questions:*

- What are some of the battles, dangers, and struggles in this world we often learn to live with and press through?

- What are some of the spiritual battles Christians face today that must *not* be ignored or treated lightly?

The devil will sneak in by any means made available to him.

Video Teaching Notes

As you watch the video teaching segment for session one, use the following outline to record anything that stands out to you. In particular, ask the Holy Spirit to help you honestly assess where you need to experience freedom and what steps you need to take to become truly free.

God's power is greater than the power of Satan!

There really are demons. However, while it's wrong thinking to believe demons are not real, it's also wrong thinking to believe Satan is behind everything.

Demons really do enter people, and they can even influence and oppress believers. There is a real danger in leaving doors open even a crack.

But Jesus really does cast demons out!

We really only have two options when it comes to demons: cast them out or leave them in.

> It is possible as believers to fail to walk in all the freedom that belongs to us.

Bible Study and Group Discussion

Take a few minutes with your group members to discuss what you just watched and explore these concepts in Scripture.

1. Tell about one great thing God has done in your life or in the life of someone you know and care about. How did God reveal His presence and power when He did this great thing?

   _____

   _____

   _____

   God's power is greater than the power of Satan!

2. **Read 1 John 4:1 – 4.** In this short passage, John refers to spirits, false prophets, and the antichrist. He is crystal clear that evil spiritual beings are at work today. Tell about how you have seen the enemy at work in the world, your community, or even your life.

   _____

   _____

   _____

3. After acknowledging the very real and present activity of evil and demonic beings, John declares with absolute confidence that "He who is in you is greater than he who is in the world" (1 John 4:4). How should this spiritual reality impact the way you view the work of the enemy in our world today?

   _____

   _____

   _____

   How have you seen the amazing and infinite power of God unleashed against the work of Satan as you have walked on your journey with Jesus?

   _____

   _____

   _____

> The promise of being set free from slavery
> is a promise to be set free completely.

4. **Read Mark 5:1 – 13.** What do you learn about the reality of the presence and work of demons in this passage?

_____

_____

What do you discover about the power and authority of Jesus in relationship to these evil spiritual beings?

_____

_____

5. There are two views of demons and the spiritual world that are equally dangerous and unhelpful: (1) demons are not real and we do not need to be concerned with them, and (2) demons are behind every struggle, problem, or tough thing we face. What are some of the unhealthy consequences associated with each of these attitudes?

_____

_____

6. What is the difference between discipleship and deliverance? Why is it essential to seek the power of Jesus for deliverance when we are dealing with demonic activity rather than simply trying to be more disciplined?

_____

_____

What possible dangers might Christians face if they are being antagonized by a demon but seek to handle the affliction with their own power?

_____

_____

> You can't disciple a demon, and you can't
> cast out the flesh! —Jack Hayford

7. **Read John 10:1–10.** During the teaching, we saw how a Christian can come under the power of a demon. What does this passage teach about how the enemy seeks to get into our hearts, minds, and lives?

How have you seen him accomplish these things in your life or the lives of people you love?

> We will never get free if we don't know
> we're in bondage in the first place.

8. None of us would ever peek out our front window, see a burglar standing at the front door, and go unlock it. We would certainly never open the door and invite the thief inside. But in a spiritual sense, this is exactly what we do with demonic influences. What are some of the ways Christians open the door of their lives to the work and ways of the enemy?

What can be done to shut the door and keep it tightly locked?

9. **Read Matthew 8:16–17 and Matthew 10:1.** What does the Bible teach about the power of Jesus to cast out demons?

What does the Bible teach about followers of Christ casting out demons in the power of Jesus' name?

10. What is one area of your life in which you feel Satan is most likely to send a demon to come knocking on your door? What can you do to keep the door shut and locked tight?

How can your group members pray for you and encourage you to stand strong against present or future efforts of the enemy to sneak into your life with the intention of stealing, killing, and destroying?

> Satan does not have the power to stop you
> from coming to Jesus.

Closing Prayer

Spend time in your group praying and calling out to God in any of the following ways:

- Ask God to help you be profoundly aware of His power and presence in your life. Pray for confidence, knowing "He who is in you is greater than he who is in the world" (1 John 4:4).

- Invite the Holy Spirit to open your eyes so you can see where the enemy is seeking to break into your life to steal, kill, and destroy.

- Confess to God where you have left the door open a crack—or all the way open—and allowed the enemy easy access to your heart, mind, and life.

- Pray for power, in the name of Jesus, to slam the door shut and keep it shut.

- Ask God to help you lift up daily prayers against the work of the enemy in your life or in the lives of those you love.

> Whenever we live by the flesh,
> we provide for the devil an opportunity
> in which he can influence us.

Between-Sessions Personal Study

Reflect further by exploring additional material from Scripture and from Truly Free.

Face the Numbers

The word *demon* appears eighty-two times in the *New King James Version* of the Bible. It occurs sixty-one times in the four Gospels alone. Look up the following passages and reflect on what they say about the reality of demons, their activity, and the power of Jesus over them.

Passage #1: Matthew 8:28–34

What does this passage say about demons?

_____
_____
_____

What does it say about the work and power of Jesus?

_____
_____
_____

How does this truth impact your spiritual life?

_____
_____
_____

Passage #2: Mark 9:17–29

What does this passage say about demons?

_____
_____
_____

What does it say about the work and power of Jesus?

_____

_____

_____

How does this truth impact your spiritual life?

_____

_____

_____

Passage #3: Luke 10:17 – 20

What does this passage say about demons?

_____

_____

_____

What does it say about the work and power of Jesus within you?

_____

_____

_____

How does this truth impact your spiritual life?

_____

_____

_____

Passage #4: Acts 19:11 – 20

What does this passage say about demons?

_____

_____

_____

Why couldn't the sons of Sceva cast out the demons?

_____

_____

_____

How does this truth impact your spiritual life?

_____

_____

_____

Passage #5: Revelation 12:7 – 9

What does this passage say about demons?

_____

_____

_____

What does it say about the power of God?

_____

_____

_____

How does this truth impact your spiritual life?

_____

_____

_____

> One of Satan's greatest strategies today is to cause people to think he doesn't exist.

Fortify Your Pastor and Church Leaders

Satan knows taking down a pastor or church leader can impact hundreds or even thousands of Christians. When a leader stumbles into sin and is caught in the enticements of the enemy, it often becomes a matter of public record, and many people find themselves discouraged in their faith. Here is the problem: every pastor and church leader is a human being with their own frailties and struggles. They need the fortification of your prayers.

1. **Write down the names** of three or four church leaders in your life. They can be pastors, board members, teachers, youth leaders.

   Name: _____

   Name: _____

   Name: _____

   Name: _____

2. **Send each one a note**, text, or email to let them know you will be praying for them for six weeks (while you are going through the *Truly Free* study). Ask if they have any particular prayer needs or areas of their life in which they need fortification and freedom. If you have a relationship with them, ask if there is a particular area of spiritual battle they are facing.

3. **Pray for these leaders** each day during this series. This will create a rhythm of prayer for six weeks. Ask God to:

   • Protect them

   • Open their eyes to places of spiritual attack and enticement

   • Give them a sense of the Holy Spirit's presence and power each day

   • Answer any specific needs they have expressed to you

4. **Check in** at the end of six weeks. Drop another note and let them know you will continue to pray for them in the coming months as the Lord brings them to your heart.

Memorize and Make It Personal

Take time to memorize 1 John 4:4:

> *You are of God, little children, and have overcome them, because He who is in you is greater than he who is in the world.*

Next, make this a personal prayer and declaration you lift up daily during the coming six weeks.

I am of God, His child, and I overcome the enemy, because
He who is in me is greater than he who is in the world!

Journal

Use the space provided below to write reflections on any of the following:

- How am I seeing and experiencing the powerful work of God in my life?

- What am I noticing about the presence of the enemy in the world and his tactics to influence culture, the church, and me?

- How am I learning to walk closer with Jesus so I can experience His power and victory in my life?

- What is the Holy Spirit saying to me through this session?

_____

_____

_____

_____

_____

_____

_____

Recommended Reading

As you reflect on and apply what God has taught you during this session, read the introduction and chapter one of *Truly Free* by Robert Morris. In preparation for the next session, read chapter two of the book. Use the space below to write any key points or questions you want to bring to the next group meeting.

_____

_____

_____

_____

_____

_____

_____

Session Two

THREE BIG WARNING SIGNS

Do not give the devil a foothold.

Ephesians 4:27 (NIV)

Introduction

Scene One: Bill and Tammy. There was a horrible grinding sound, followed by a loud thud, and then the car drifted to a stop. It was a good thing Tammy was driving on a residential street when the engine seized and shut down. When her husband, Bill, arrived, he asked, as gently as he knew how, "Were there any signs, lights on the dashboard, or hints something might be wrong with the car?" She looked down at the ground as she reported, "For the last couple of weeks there was a red light on and the car has been making some funny sounds."

Scene Two: Kenny and Lisa. The emotional temperature in Kenny and Lisa's marriage ranged from cold to frigid. Conversations were short and many ended with Lisa feeling hurt and frustrated. Intimacy was becoming rare. When Kenny came home late from work one night, and the house was dark and empty, he was confused. When he found the letter from Lisa explaining she would be staying with her parents for a few weeks to "sort things out," he still did not really get what was happening. In his mind, things in their marriage were going "pretty good."

Scene Three: Benedict. The pains in Benedict's chest seemed to pop up once or twice a week. Sometimes they came paired with tension in his arms and shortness of breath. He figured it was probably indigestion. Maybe it was just normal pain that came with stress. He had always had a high threshold for pain, and he prided himself on how he could "tough it out and press through" most of the hard things in life. He never had any idea what hit him until he woke up in the hospital after quadruple bypass surgery. Benedict's first words when he regained consciousness were, "How did I get here?"

Life is full of warning signs. When we ignore them or miss them, the consequences are almost always more serious than we would have guessed. This is true in every area of our lives ... but most of all, in our spiritual lives.

> It is possible for us to give the enemy
> "footholds" in our lives.

Talk About It

To get things started for this second session, discuss one of the following questions:

- Tell about a time you missed a warning sign. It might have been as literal as a "BRIDGE OUT" sign or as subtle as an emotional signal someone was trying to give you. What sign did you miss, and what were the consequences?

- What is one clearly posted warning sign God has placed in the Bible that some people today drive right past?

> If the trouble in our lives has a spiritual root,
> then Jesus can easily deliver us
> and take care of the spiritual root.

Video Teaching Notes

As you watch the video teaching segment for session two, use the following outline to record anything that stands out to you. In particular, ask the Holy Spirit to help you honestly assess where you need to experience freedom and what steps you need to take to become truly free.

There are three big warning signs that alert us to demonic bondage in our lives. Warning sign #1 is **continued iniquity.** This is a sin you keep going back to again and again.

_____

_____

_____

_____

When we formulate a plan to stay in sin, we are in bondage.

We can say we've been delivered, but if we are continuing in sin we are still in bondage.

Warning sign #2 is **continued illness.** Illness itself is not an indicator that a person has a demon or has sin in his or her life. However, if a person has continued illnesses, there is a *possibility* there is a spiritual battle behind it.

In Luke 13:11–16, Jesus healed a woman who had been bound by a spirit of infirmity for eighteen years. Jesus said she was a "daughter of Abraham"—she was a Jew who had faith in God—yet she was still bound by this evil spirit. The same can be true of us.

Warning sign #3 is **continued influence.** There is a real danger of "dabbling" in the occult, because this opens a door for the enemy.

Jesus said deliverance is not for the lost but for the children of God.

_____

_____

_____

_____

Bondage begins when we believe a lie.

Bible Study and Group Discussion

Take a few minutes with your group members to discuss what you just watched and explore these concepts in Scripture.

1. Since the last session of *Truly Free,* you have been reflecting on the reality that demons do exist and can influence believers. In what ways have you seen people (yourself included, if that's the case) open the door to this damaging spiritual control?

_____

_____

When we undertake certain activities, the devil is given legal grounds to claim his turf.

2. **Read John 8:31–36.** Jesus is talking to believers, yet He tells them they need to be set free. What are some of the things Christians today, in your particular community, need to be set free from? What are some of the common forms of bondage people might not even notice or identify as a spiritual battle?

_____

_____

_____

3. Christians who set their heart on a sin (formulate a plan) and continue in that sin (keep doing it over and over) will end up in bondage. What are some examples of how believers can "plan to sin" and "continue in it" while still thinking they are free?

_____

_____

_____

> When you find yourself saying, "God,
> I'll never do that again," about the same sin,
> over and over … this is continued iniquity.

4. Instead of planning to sin, we should be formulating a plan to get out from under the influence of sin. What specific steps can we take to identify where we are in bondage and break the chains of harmful spiritual influences?

_____

_____

_____

> Don't stand in God's house and say, "I am delivered."
> Come to God's house, confess your sin, and get delivered.

5. **Read Luke 13:10 – 16.** It's important to remember the Bible does *not* teach if people are sick they have a demon or even that they have opened up the door to sin in their life. However, if people have a continuing illness, there is a *possibility* a spiritual battle is behind it. What implications do we face if we declare *every* sickness is a matter of demonic activity or sin in a person's life?

_____

_____

_____

On the other hand, why is it wise to recognize that continued illness *could* be a sign a person is in a spiritual battle?

6. In the video, Pastor Morris explains how he experienced an unusual amount of physical accidents during his life. He finally realized he had been believing a lie, and this wrong attitude had opened the door for spiritual attack. Tell about a lie you believed that led to spiritual attack in your life. How did knowing the truth—and believing the truth—set you free from the power of the lie the enemy was speaking to you?

7. **Read Mark 7:24–30.** The woman in this story had been influenced by two sinful attitudes that saturated her culture: pride and openness to the occult. Why is it critical to identify harmful spiritual patterns and strongholds that exist in our family, our culture, and even our nationality of origin?

   How have you seen a sinful pattern that exists in your family, culture, or nationality of origin begin to creep into your life? How have you battled against it?

8. **Read Deuteronomy 18:9–12.** Occult behavior has become commonplace in many parts of the world. What are some of the subtle and obvious occult practices that have crept into our world today?

What are some possible dangers and consequences if a follower of Jesus dabbles in these practices (even when they might seem benign or harmless)?

_____

_____

_____

9. The pathway to true freedom is humbly coming to Jesus and asking for His deliverance and power over the enemy. When was a time you cried out to Jesus to deliver you and He showed up and set you free?

_____

_____

_____

> As believers we can either choose to walk in slavery and be in bondage, or we can choose to walk in the Sonship He has given us.

10. What causes us to resist running to Jesus even when we realize (or suspect) we are under attack or in bondage?

_____

_____

_____

What needs to change in our hearts, attitudes, or understandings to help us run to Jesus when we have even a slight suspicion we are under demonic attack or influence?

_____

_____

_____

> You're going to serve somebody, and whomever you serve is going to be a master over you.

Closing Prayer

Spend time in your group praying and calling out to God in any of the following ways:

- Thank God for giving you warning signs to help you see when the enemy is seeking to attack and influence your life.

- Pray for humility to see when you are under attack, discernment to realize the source of the attack, and wisdom to know how to resist in the power of Jesus.

- Confess where there is continued iniquity in your life and ask for the power of the Holy Spirit to help you turn from this sin.

- If you (or a loved one) are dealing with continued illness, pray for eyes to see if there might be some form of spiritual attack behind it.

- Ask God to make you aware of any occult practices you are dabbling in or diving into that are opening the door to damaging spiritual influence in your life.

Don't make plans to sin. Make plans to run from sin.

Between-Sessions Personal Study

Reflect further by exploring additional material from Scripture and from Truly Free.

Fortify Your Mind

We all have family and cultural influences that can impact our spiritual lives in negative ways, and for this reason we all need to retrain our minds and our thinking. Take time today to memorize the following three short passages, and allow them to become part of your thinking on a deep and personal level.

Passage #1: 1 John 4:4

> *You are of God, little children, and have overcome [evil spirits], because He who is in you is greater than he who is in the world.*

Write what this passage means for you as you stand strong against any work of the enemy in your life:

_____

_____

_____

_____

_____

Passage #2: James 4:7

> *Therefore submit to God. Resist the devil and he will flee from you.*

Write what this passage means for you as you stand strong against any work of the enemy in your life:

_____
_____
_____
_____
_____

Passage #3: Ephesians 6:17

> *Take the helmet of salvation, and the sword of the Spirit,*
> *which is the word of God.*

Write what this passage means for you as you stand strong against any work of the enemy in your life:

_____
_____
_____
_____
_____

> If we have any manner of thinking contrary
> to God's Word, then it's an open door to the devil.

Read the Signs

In this session, we talked about three warning signs that can alert us to potential places of spiritual attack and bondage. They are:

1. Continued Iniquity
2. Continued Illness
3. Continued Influence

Remember, Christians do not have to be paranoid and see a demon behind every bush, but we need to be aware we have a real enemy who is always seeking to steal, kill, and destroy. Following are two easy-to-remember "warning signs" to remind yourself of the spiritual battles around you. Use the space provided to create a couple more simple warning signs that you might find helpful to your own situations

Sign: *If you know it is wrong, don't do it!*

Sign: *Warning: Lion Ahead (1 Peter 5:8)*

Sign: _____

_____

_____

Sign: _____

_____

_____

Sign: _____

_____

Put some of your customized warning signs in places where you'll see them regularly. This could be a pop-up note in your phone that comes up once or twice a day or a handwritten sign on your refrigerator or on your bathroom mirror. Just be discreet—these warnings are designed for you and others might not understand what they mean.

Family History Study

In this session we've seen how our cultural and family backgrounds can have a great impact on us, so today take time to study your own family background. Interview three family members who have memories of your family that go further back than you can remember. Or, if you have a written family history, review it. Write some notes from your findings on the following pages.

Interview 1: *What I Learned*

What are some great examples of faith in my family that inspired me?

What patterns of continued iniquity and sinful behaviors have marked my family history?

What patterns of sickness, injuries, and various kinds of illness are part of my family history?

What patterns of engagement in negative spiritual behavior (even the occult) have marked my family?

Interview 2: *What I Learned*

What are some great examples of faith in my family that inspired me?

What patterns of continued iniquity and sinful behaviors have marked my family history?

What patterns of sickness, injuries, and various kinds of illness are part of my family history?

_____

_____

_____

What patterns of engagement in negative spiritual behavior (even the occult) have marked my family?

_____

_____

_____

Interview 3: *What I Learned*

What are some great examples of faith in my family that inspired me?

_____

_____

_____

What patterns of continued iniquity and sinful behaviors have marked my family history?

_____

_____

_____

What patterns of sickness, injuries, and various kinds of illness are part of my family history?

_____

_____

_____

What patterns of engagement in negative spiritual behavior (even the occult) have marked my family?

_____

_____

_____

Journal

Use the space provided below to write reflections on any of the following questions:

- What are patterns of continued iniquity that can crop up in my life?

- How have I battled these in the past, and how can I resist these in the future?

- What are ways the enemy has attacked me or my family members in terms of health, accidents, or other physical challenges?

- How can I battle against these and stand strong in the power of Jesus?

- What are specific influences I need to be aware of and intentionally resist?

- What can I do to stand against these influences and make sure they don't impact my life?

- What is the Holy Spirit saying to me through this session?

Recommended Reading

In preparation for the next session, read chapter three of *Truly Free*. Use the space below to write any key points or questions you want to bring to the next group meeting.

Session Three

BEWARE THE CHALDEANS

I have forgiven in the sight of Christ for your sake, in order that Satan might not outwit us. For we are not unaware of his schemes.

2 CORINTHIANS 2:10–11 (NIV)

Introduction

Ask any professional athlete, or even a college-level athlete, and they will say the same thing. When they are preparing to compete against another team, they always watch film and review the strategy of their opponent. They gather every legal and legitimate bit of data they can find. They study, dissect, and evaluate. They analyze their rival's plays, past games, and patterns.

They would be fools not to do so; their goal is to win. And so these athletes and their coach staffs spend countless hours crunching data because they know the more they understand the thinking and tactics of their opponent, the better chance they have of winning.

Think about it. Christians are not playing a game, but we are in a real spiritual battle that has life-and-death consequences. We are not looking for a "win" when the buzzer sounds and the competition is over; we are seeking to honor and exalt the Maker of heaven and earth. We are not engaged in a sporting contest; we are seeking to live for the glory of God. We are not participating in a match that ends with us shaking the opponent's hand; we are in a spiritual battle with principalities and powers that are unyielding in their commitment to destroy us.

It is time for followers of Jesus to take this battle seriously. We need to study the enemy's tactics, look at his playbook, and analyze his patterns. If we dig into the Bible and study intensely, we will discover God has given us insight into the plans and strategies of Satan and his demonic workers. We must commit ourselves to learn all we can about the evil one and prepare to fight back with wisdom, insight, and the weapons of spiritual warfare.

> We need to know how our enemy works so
> we can recognize the battles and win the fight.

Talk About It

To get things started for this third session, discuss one of the following questions:

- What can we learn from athletes and coaches when it comes to their tenacious commitment to study their opponent before engaging in a competition?

- Why is it so important for Christians to study their opponent and be prepared for the spiritual battles we all will face?

> Being vigilant means to be watchful.
> It means we are not afraid of Satan and we're not unaware of his schemes.

Video Teaching Notes

As you watch the video teaching segment for session three, use the following outline to record anything that stands out to you. In particular, ask the Holy Spirit to help you honestly assess where you need to experience freedom and what steps you need to take to become truly free.

God described the Chaldeans as a "bitter and hasty nation which marches through the breadth of the earth, to possess dwelling places that are not theirs" (Habakkuk 1:6). Chaldeans represent demons that blind us to truth that makes us free.

There are three things we need to know about the Chaldeans. First, they are **thieves**. They come to steal (1) our minds, (2) our money, and (3) our morals.

Second, the Chaldeans are **vicious**, like wolves. They size us up, learning our movements and weaknesses, and then alert the rest of the pack.

Third, the Chaldeans are **cunning**. They try to distract us, deceive us, and determine our futures for us. They are like fishermen, planning what bait and hooks they are going to use to catch us.

There are three ways we battle the Chaldeans. First, we stay **sober**, or self-controlled.

A second way to battle the Chaldeans is to stay **close to other sheep**. Demons are looking for those who are isolated, so it's important to surround ourselves with other believers.

A third way to battle the Chaldeans is to **run to the Shepherd**. David says, "Your rod and Your staff, they comfort me" (Psalm 23:4). The Shepherd doesn't use the rod on the sheep but on the wolves! This is why the rod and staff comfort us.

> The biggest solution to spiritual oppression
> is to stay close to the Shepherd.

Bible Study and Group Discussion

Take a few minutes with your group members to discuss what you just watched and explore these concepts in Scripture.

1. Sometimes, when we are behind closed doors, Satan attacks us the most. How have you experienced this reality that temptation and enticement to sin seem to come more intensely when we are isolated, alone, or away from home?

What can we do to fortify ourselves and create spiritual accountability and support, even when life situations make us feel alone and vulnerable?

2. **Read Acts 13:40–41** and **Habakkuk 1:5–6.** The Chaldeans were a real people who existed at a real time in history. What were some of the characteristics that marked this nation? How did they treat other nations and people groups?

In 539 BC, the Persians defeated the Chaldeans, and they disappeared from human history. Later, the term "Chaldeans" came to refer to demons. How do demons demonstrate some of the same characteristics and behaviors as the Chaldeans?

3. Some people say just as there are no more Chaldeans, there are no more demons. What are some of the dangerous consequences we will face if we deny the presence and activity of demons in the world today?

> Make no mistake—Satan is vicious and his bunch is vicious. They never have a good day.

4. **Read John 10:7–10, Habakkuk 1:6,** and **Matthew 12:43–45.** Satan and his demonic workers are thieves. They always steal and take possession of what is not theirs. What does Jesus say about the enemy and how he steals?

How have you seen this reality in your life or in the life of someone you love?

_____

_____

_____

5. One of the things the enemy and his minions love to steal is the next generation. How do you see Satan and his workers influencing, capturing, and enticing the next generation to draw them away from Jesus?

_____

_____

_____

How can parents, grandparents, other family, and Christian friends reach out to young people and speak truth, extend love, and point them back to Jesus?

_____

_____

_____

6. There are three things the enemy seeks to steal from God's people: our _minds_, our _money_, and our _morals_. In what ways right now is the enemy seeking to steal one of these from you? How can your group pray for you and encourage you to fight the battle you are facing?

_____

_____

_____

7. **Read Habakkuk 1:7–9.** In the video you learned some of the ways wolves behave, size up their enemy, and attack their prey. How do you see Satan and his demonic workers hunting and attacking believers today? What tactics do you see the enemy using with effectiveness in today's world and culture?

_____

_____

_____

8. One of the ways the enemy picks off sheep is to isolate them and get them away from the flock. What are some of the dangers that come when a believer gets out of the habit of being in regular fellowship, gathered worship, and support groups with other Christians?

How are we protected and strengthened when we commit to deep levels of Christian community?

> The people of God act as a buffer between us and the enemy. A sheep that's off to himself, away from the pack, is open to attack. The solution is insulation, not isolation.

9. **Read Daniel 2:1–2, Habakkuk 1:15, and Ephesians 6:10–13.** Our enemy is a tricky, cunning, schemer! He lives to distract, deceive, and destroy our future. He dangles a lure in front of us with whatever bait he thinks will entice us. What bait do you have to beware of and fight to avoid? How can your group members pray for you and keep you accountable to avoid these specific temptations?

10. **Read 1 Peter 5:8–9 and Revelation 5:4–5.** Scripture warns that our adversary, the devil, prowls around like a lion looking for people to devour. What are ways we can stay sharp, keep sober, and be on the watch for the work of the enemy?

Yet the Bible says there is another lion: Jesus, the Lion of the tribe of Judah. He has prevailed and is victorious! Why is it critical that we run to Jesus all the time—especially when the enemy is on the prowl? What are ways we can run to Jesus and stay close to Him?

> Being sober means we are in control of ourselves through the power of the Holy Spirit.

Closing Prayer

Spend time in your group praying and calling out to God in any of the following ways:

- Ask God to help you take the spiritual battles you face more seriously than you have been taking them in the past.

- Confess where you have been enticed by the enemy and ask for forgiveness and a repentant heart.

- Invite the Holy Spirit to open your eyes to see where the enemy is at work. Pray for awareness, but not a fearful spirit.

- Pray for the next generation and ask God to protect and fortify them to fight the enemy with heavenly strength.

- Tell God you want to be a sheep who runs to the Good Shepherd and stays near Him at all times.

> If you're feeling oppressed by evil, then run to the Shepherd. Run to the Lord!

Between-Sessions
Personal Study

Reflect further by exploring additional material from Scripture and from Truly Free.

Playbook

Satan keeps using the same playbook *because it keeps working.* For this reason, we need to become familiar with his tactics so we can fight back. Take time today to read a few passages in the Bible that reveal these tactics of the enemy and his demonic workers. List each tactic that you find.

Passage #1: Genesis 3:1–13

Tactics of the enemy:

_____

_____

_____

_____

_____

How you can fight back against these specific tactics:

_____

_____

_____

_____

_____

_____

Passage #2: Matthew 4:1 – 11

Tactics of the enemy:

How you can fight back against these specific tactics:

Passage #3: 2 Corinthians 11:3 – 15

Tactics of the enemy:

How you can fight back against these specific tactics:

> Satan is never merciful. When a person
> has a tough time or goes through a tragedy in his life,
> that's when Satan attacks his hardest.

Fill Your House

In Matthew 12:43–45, Jesus teaches this:

> *When an unclean spirit goes out of a man, he goes through dry places, seeking rest, and finds none. Then he says, "I will return to my house from which I came." And when he comes, he finds it empty, swept, and put in order. Then he goes and takes with him seven other spirits more wicked than himself, and they enter and dwell there; and the last state of that man is worse than the first. So shall it also be with this wicked generation.*

One word that should jump out of this passage and grab our hearts is "empty." This house was left unoccupied. It is a picture of a person who has been delivered from a demonic presence but has failed to be filled with the Holy Spirit and the things of God.

Take time in the coming days to reflect on things you should fill your house (your life) with. Seek to have your heart, life, and time so filled with the things of God that there is no room for the enemy to slither in. Here are some suggestions to get you started. Add some extra items to the list and spend time filling up with the things of God.

- The **Holy Spirit:** Pray for fresh filling and surrender to the Spirit's leading.

- The **Word of God:** Read it, memorize passages, and reflect deeply on biblical truth.

- **Worship:** Sing, praise, and celebrate God with frequency and passion. Make weekly worship with God's people a high priority.

- **Fellowship:** Make time to be with God's people, share meals, talk about your journey of faith, and encourage each other.

- **Service:** Love, care, and serve others in the name of Jesus.

-

-

-

Identify the Thief and Set an Alarm

Many of us have alarm systems in our homes and even on our cars. We know the world is a broken place and there are thieves who would love to take what does not belong to them. So we identify places where there could be a threat and set an alarm.

Yet it is much more important for us to identify the *spiritual thief* and set alarms to alert us when he is attempting to take what is not his. In this session we learned the enemy wants to steal our minds, our money, and our morals. Use the space provided to identify ways you think the enemy might try to steal each of these. Then write down a few ways you will know this is happening and how you will respond in the power of Jesus.

Ways the enemy might seek to steal *my mind, thinking, attitudes, and motives:*

How will I know this is happening? What will set off my "discernment alarm" and move me to action?

What action will I take when I know the enemy is seeking to steal from me?

Ways the enemy might seek to steal *my money, resources, energy to work, and material goods God has placed in my care:*

How will I know this is happening? What will set off my "discernment alarm" and move me to action?

What action will I take when I know the enemy is seeking to steal from me?

Ways the enemy might seek to steal *my morals, character, holiness, and desire to honor Jesus each day:*

How will I know this is happening? What will set off my "discernment alarm" and move me to action?

What action will I take when I know the enemy is seeking to steal from me?

_____

_____

_____

_____

Journal

Use the space provided below to write reflections on any of the following questions:

- What are some of the primary tactics the enemy tends to use against me?

- How can I resist these tactics?

- What tactics do I see the enemy using against my family members and friends?

- How can I warn these people or help them identify what tactics are being used against them?

- How can I fortify my life against the attacks of the enemy?

- What can I do, on a daily basis, to run to Jesus, my Great Shepherd, and make sure I stay close to Him?

- What is the Holy Spirit saying to me through this session?

_____

_____

_____

_____

_____

_____

_____

_____

_____

_____

_____

_____

_____

_____

_____

_____

_____

_____

_____

_____

_____

_____

Recommended Reading

In preparation for the next session, read chapter four of _Truly Free_. Use the space below to write any key points or questions you want to bring to the next group meeting.

_____

_____

_____

_____

_____

_____

_____

_____

Session Four

BREAKING THE
SNARE OF PRIDE

Pride goes before destruction, and a haughty spirit before a fall.

Proverbs 16:18

Introduction

In 2007, *Are You Smarter Than a Fifth Grader?* launched to American television audiences. The premise of the game show was simple and intriguing: Bring in some adults, ask them questions that show up in the educational curriculum of the normal fifth-grade student, pit these adults against some fifth graders, and then watch them squirm!

Viewers tuned in to laugh, learn fifth-grade stuff they had forgotten, and watch the drama unfold. The show was so popular it ran for a number of years and was even picked up in the international TV market. Why was it so dramatic and compelling? The answer is quite simple: many adults could not answer the questions. There are lots of bright and informed grown-ups who simply don't know what a fifth grader knows about certain topics.

Here's another question: *Are you smarter than God?* This might sound like a ridiculous question to ask, but it is an important one for us to consider. If many adults can't beat fifth graders in a simple trivia game show, why in the world would they think they are smarter than God?

Most people would say, "Of course I am not smarter than God." But when we trust in ourselves more than the Lord—when we rely on our own intellect, strength, righteousness, or wisdom—we are acting as if we are smarter than the Creator of heaven and earth. When pride takes over, we begin to trust in ourselves. This attitude kicks open the door for Satan and his demonic workers to come in and make our lives their playground.

> When we compare ourselves to God,
> none of us measure up.

Talk About It

To get things started for this fourth session, discuss one of the following questions:

- What are some of the ways people today act as if they are smarter than God?

- What are some of God's commands and teachings people have decided are no longer worth following? How is this a sign of pride?

> Sometimes we can feel inadequate
> because we feel adequate ... in ourselves.

Video Teaching Notes

As you watch the video teaching segment for session four, use the following outline to record anything that stands out to you. In particular, ask the Holy Spirit to help you honestly assess where you need to experience freedom and what steps you need to take to become truly free.

Pride opens doors we don't want open and blinds us to our own sin.

There are three ways we can identify pride. First, pride is **trusting in our own strength.** In Luke 22:31–32, Jesus said Satan had demanded *and received permission* to attack Peter, because he was trusting in his own strength.

What we can learn from Peter's mistakes ...

Second, pride is **trusting in our own righteousness**. In the story of Job, we find Job saying over and over again he's done nothing wrong and he's righteous. It seems Job was trusting in his own righteousness instead of the Lord's, and in this way he opened the door to the enemy.

What we can learn from Job's mistakes ...

Third, pride is **trusting in our own wisdom.** In 1 Kings 22:19–23, we read the Lord "put a lying spirit" in the mouths of King Ahab's prophets. Why? Because Ahab trusted in his own wisdom and thought he knew what was best.

What we can learn from Ahab's mistakes ...

God gives Satan permission to come against us because He knows pride will destroy us. God, in His grace, allows the enemy to attack us so we will come to repentance and be saved.

_____

_____

_____

_____

> When we trust in our own strength, righteousness, and wisdom, we open the door to the work of the enemy.

Bible Study and Group Discussion

Take a few minutes with your group members to discuss what you just watched and explore these concepts in Scripture.

1. Pride is trusting in our own **strength**, **righteousness**, and **wisdom**. But pride goes well beyond these three categories. Pride rears its ugly head and invites in the enemy any time we trust ourselves more than we trust God. What can pride look like in people's lives when they have one of the follow attitudes?

   I trust in my *sense of right and wrong* more than what God says in *His Word* ...

   _____

   _____

   _____

   I trust in my *decisions for the future* more than *God's leading and direction* ...

   _____

   _____

   _____

I trust in my *resourcefulness* more than *God's provision* ...

Pride opens the door to spiritual attack.

2. **Read Luke 22:31–34** and **Mark 14:27–31.** What was the nature of Peter's pride? How could this sinful attitude become a doorway for spiritual attack in his life?

3. Jesus emphatically told Peter he would deny Him before the night was done. But Peter looked at Jesus and, with passion and conviction, said, "You are wrong!" There are times when we read the Bible, hear God speak, and say, "God, you are wrong!" What are examples of ways we disagree with God? How does the enemy use these against us?

It seems like everyone who has pride in their lives can't see it is there.

4. **Read Matthew 16:21–23.** Jesus declared he would die on the cross and rise again. As we look back at this moment in history, we know Jesus' sacrifice was the only way our sins could be washed away. When Peter, in his own strength, tried to stop Jesus from going to the cross, he had no idea what he was talking about. What implications would it have had on humanity if Peter had gotten his way and

Jesus hadn't gone to the cross?

Because God's strength won — and Jesus *did* go to the cross and rise again — what results has that had on human history?

> ## Righteous living does not make us righteous.
> ## Only the blood of Jesus Christ does.

5. **Read Job 1:6–12.** What do you learn in this passage about God's power and authority over Satan? How do you respond to the idea that God gave the enemy permission to come against Job?

6. **Read Job 32:1–2, 33:8–9, 36:3,** and **40:8.** In this session we learned Job was a righteous man, but he had become proud of his righteousness. What is the difference between being a righteous person through the grace of God and trusting in our own righteousness?

What attitudes and behaviors begin to slip into our lives when we become self-righteous?

7. *Our trust is in Christ and Christ alone.* What has Jesus done to prove He is trustworthy? How can we find true and eternal righteousness in Jesus alone?

How can keeping our eyes on Jesus and the cross become an antidote to self-righteousness?

8. **Read 1 Kings 22:7 – 8** and **22:19 – 23.** These passages can seem shocking and troublesome, because it appears God is working against Ahab and bringing disaster to his life. But shift gears for a moment and think about a loving parent. What are some of the reasons a caring and responsible parent might discipline a child?

When God sees one of His children trusting in their own wisdom, He knows disaster is on the horizon. What are some of the means God might use to bring a child to a place of repentance and humility? How are each of these means, ultimately, an act of compassionate love from a heavenly Father?

9. God allowed Peter, Job, and Ahab to come under attack. Think about how each of their stories ends. How does repentance and a humble heart lead to healing and hope? How does resistance and refusal to respond to God's discipline lead to serious consequences?

> Could it be God allows us to come under attack
> so we will repent and humbly run back to Him?

10. Which of these areas of pride are you most tempted to wander into: Trusting your own strength? Trusting your own righteousness? Trusting your own wisdom? Why do you think that is so?

_____

_____

_____

How can you battle against this, repent, and run to God with a humble heart? How can your group members pray for you and encourage you as you address this area of potential pride?

_____

_____

_____

> The straightforward solution to the problem
> of pride is to always depend on the Lord.

Closing Prayer

Spend time in your group praying and calling out to God in any of the following ways:

- Confess the temptation we all feel to trust in our own strength.

- Ask God to help you trust in His power and strength rather than in your own.

- Invite the Holy Spirit to show you when and where you are trusting in yourself and not in God.

- Pray that God will help you see if you are slipping into an attitude of religious self-righteousness.

- Thank Jesus for purchasing your righteousness on the cross and offering it to you freely.

- Declare your confidence that only Jesus' righteousness is enough to cleanse you and set you free ... for eternity.

- Invite the Holy Spirit to help you grow in godly wisdom and give you strength to always trust in God's wisdom.

Between-Sessions
Personal Study

Reflect further by exploring additional material from Scripture and from Truly Free.

The Rest of the Story

Read the rest of Peter's, Job's, and Ahab's stories in the Bible and take notes on how they responded to the conflicts they faced because of their pride. Also look at how their stories end.

Story #1: Peter

Read John 21:1–19. How did Peter respond after realizing his sinfulness?

Read Acts 2–4. How did Peter's story end?

Story #2: Job

Read Job 40:4–5 and Job 42:2–6. How did Job respond to God's rebuke?

Read Job 42:7–17. How does Job's story end?

Story #3: Ahab

Read 1 Kings 21:17–22:28. How did Ahab respond to God's rebuke?

Read 1 Kings 22:29–40. How does Ahab's story end?

How did the story end for those who exhibited repentance and humility? How did the story end for the one who continued in pride and resisted God?

Preventive Measures

Take time in the coming twenty-four hours to memorize this one simple verse:

> *Pride goes before destruction, and a haughty spirit*
> *before a fall.*

Proverbs 16:18

Don't use this verse as something to quote against those who seem a bit arrogant. Instead, let it motivate you to come humbly before God and invite the Holy Spirit to search your heart. Once you have memorized this verse, add a second layer of self-challenge.

Read Psalm 139. Notice David (a man who knew a bit about self-deception, sin, and consequences) begins by declaring, "O Lord, You have searched me and known me." He goes on to relate all the things God knows about him:

You know my sitting down and my rising up;
You understand my thought afar off.
You comprehend my path and my lying down,
And are acquainted with all my ways.
For there is not a word on my tongue,
But behold, O LORD, You know it altogether ...
You formed my inward parts;
You covered me in my mother's womb.
I will praise You, for I am fearfully and wonderfully made;
Marvelous are Your works,
And that my soul knows very well.
My frame was not hidden from You,
When I was made in secret,
And skillfully wrought in the lowest parts of the earth.
Your eyes saw my substance, being yet unformed.
And in Your book they all were written,
The days fashioned for me,
When as yet there were none of them.

(vv. 2–4, 13–16)

Close by joining David in this passionate prayer:

Search me, O God, and know my heart;
Try me, and know my anxieties;
And see if there is any wicked way in me,
And lead me in the way everlasting.

(vv. 23–24)

Pride is a foothold the devil loves.
He loves it because it's so sneaky to detect.

A Life-Saving Decision ... Repent!

During this session we've talked a lot about repenting. When God allows Satan to attack us, in order to save us from destruction, the best response is to repent! When we realize we have become prideful and are living with the consequences, we need to repent! When sin is slipping in quietly, and it does not seem like a big deal, and we think we can handle it, we need to repent. To do this, we must identify the sin that has crept in. We must name it for what it is—prideful rebellion—and turn around and run. We need to change our attitudes and actions. We must humble ourselves. Use the space below to help you navigate this process:

Identify: *Name the specific sin that has crept into your life ...*

Confess: *Tell God you are sorry for your sin ...*

Repent: *Cry out to God for the power to change, and make a conscious decision to turn from this sin. Describe what action you need to take ...*

Journal

Use the space provided below to write reflections on any of the following questions:

- How do I tend to trust in my own strength?

- When am I most tempted to do this? How can I resist this temptation?

- How am I trusting my own strength now? What must I do to repent?

- How do I tend to trust in my own righteousness?

- When am I most tempted to do this? How can I resist this temptation?

- How am I trusting my own righteousness now? What must I do to repent?

- How do I tend to trust in my own wisdom?

- When am I most tempted to do this? How can I resist this temptation?

- How am I trusting my own wisdom now? What must I do to repent?

- What is the Holy Spirit saying to me through this session?

Recommended Reading

In preparation for the next session, read chapter seven of *Truly Free*. Use the space below to write any key points or questions you want to bring to the next group meeting.

Session Five

BREAKING THE
SNARE OF LUST

*Put on the Lord Jesus Christ, and make no provision for the
flesh, to fulfill its lusts.*

Romans 13:14

Introduction

Cause and effect. It is a simple idea we see played out in a thousand ways every day. Think about it. Almost everything has some kind of consequences associated with it.

A little boy sits at the dinner table, and Mom says, "Honey, eat your green beans or there will be no dessert for you." Cause and effect.

A teenage girl finally gets her license after classes, practice, and a trip to the Department of Motor Vehicles. She decides the speed limit is more of a suggestion than a hard-and-fast rule. Then the flashing lights in her rearview mirror and the ear-piercing sound of a siren wake her up to reality. Ten minutes later she is back on the road with a ticket in her glove box. Ten days later she is facing the reality that her insurance just went through the roof. Cause and effect.

A couple goes on vacation and decides, for the next week, they won't think much about exercise or how much they eat. It's their vacation after all, and they just want to have fun. After seven days of eating about five meals a day, they get home and decide to step on the scale. Let's just say they were both shocked. Cause and effect.

A husband takes a business trip to Las Vegas. He actually believes the commercial he saw on TV: "What happens in Vegas stays in Vegas." He is away from home, his family, his church, and any sense of accountability. The lights, glitz, and parade of women ready to party catch his attention. Lust begins to simmer as he walks around the casinos. For just a few days he drops his guard, feeds the lust, and ignores the warnings the Holy Spirit is speaking into his heart. When he arrives home he feels deep guilt and shame. But he keeps telling himself his actions and decisions for those "few little days" were *not that big of a deal, no one will ever know,* and what happened in Vegas *will certainly stay there and not impact his future.* He has covered his tracks … or so he thinks. Then, a couple of weeks later, the inevitable happens. Cause and effect.

Did you know God has a wonderful plan for your life?
The problem is Satan has a plan as well.

Talk About It

To get things started for this fifth session, discuss one of the following questions:

- In the final scenario from the introduction, what are some of the ways the "Vegas story" could end? What are some of the cause-and-effect consequences that might surface in this man's heart, life, marriage, family, and faith?

- What was a cause-and-effect experience you faced when you made a decision or took an action that was sinful and "secret"? How did you later have to face the consequences?

Sin always has consequences.

Video Teaching Notes

As you watch the video teaching segment for session five, use the following outline to record anything that stands out to you. In particular, ask the Holy Spirit to help you honestly assess where you need to experience freedom and what steps you need to take to become truly free.

Lust is one of the most deceptive and serious tactics the enemy is using against this generation.

_____

_____

_____

_____

There are four things to know about the snare of lust. First, God gave us **desires** and a context in which those desires can be satisfied, but anything outside that context will lead to sin.

Second, lust always brings a **deception.** Lust tries to deceive us by saying there is something better than what God has for us, but the truth is lust can *never* be satisfied.

Lust always leads to **death.** Perhaps this will not be physical death but the death of a marriage, or the death of a family, or even the death of a person's creativity.

The solution to the snare of lust is **deliverance** and **discipleship.** Note that we need *both*.

Strongholds can be positive or negative—they can refer to a fortress, a prison, or a tomb. The Lord is our fortress, but lust is a wrong fortress that becomes a prison and leads to the tomb.

Strongholds are trains of thought. Our destinies depend on which train we board.

Lust promises benefit but brings only heartache.

Bible Study and Group Discussion

Take a few minutes with your group members to discuss what you just watched and explore these concepts in Scripture.

1. The snare of lust is one of the most subtle and deceiving spirits we will face, and this sinful enticement is one of the most serious battles our generation is facing. What are some of the ways our world has changed in the past two decades because of lust? How have these changes made lusting easier and more acceptable for many people?

2. **Read Proverbs 7:6–27.** Solomon tells about looking out his window and seeing a destructive drama play out right in front of his eyes. As you look at the passage, there are several things you can learn about the enticement of lust. Respond to *one or two* of the following questions:

   What poor choice did this man make about *location* ... where he went?

What mistake did he make when it came to *when* he wandered to this place?

_____

_____

What do you see in the woman's *attitude* that was dangerous and damaging?

_____

_____

How does this story paint a wrong *view of religion*?

_____

_____

How does it portray a twisted understanding of *love*?

_____

_____

The woman assured the man they *wouldn't get caught* because her husband was far away. How is this lie repeated over and over when lust is present?

_____

_____

When the man yielded to the temptation, there were *consequences*... cause and effect. What were these consequences?

_____

_____

The spirit of lust robs us of wisdom and understanding.

3. This passage in Proverbs operates on two distinct and interlocking levels. First, it was most likely a real scene that Solomon witnessed involving a man and a woman. But it is also a window into the spiritual world. As we look at this woman, we can see a picture of the tactics of the spirit of lust. Look at this biblical text through spiritual eyes and make a list of the **specific strategies** the spirit of lust uses to lure, entice, and destroy people.

- _____
  _____
- _____
  _____
- _____
  _____
- _____
  _____
- _____
  _____
- _____

Now pick at least one of these strategies. How can you identify it and battle against it?

_____
_____
_____

4. **Read Romans 13:14.** When unhealthy desires crop up that are driven by lust, the enemy wants us to focus on them, fixate on them, and eventually seek to fulfill them. In what ways can we fixate on lustful desires and even make plans to act on them?

_____
_____
_____

What can we do to block the sources of lust-producing desires and train ourselves to run from lustful thoughts?

_____
_____
_____

Do whatever is necessary to avoid evil.

5. **Read Proverbs 6:23–33, Proverbs 27:20, and Ezekiel 16:28.** Lust is like a black hole. It can't be filled, it is never satisfied, and it always wants more. The enemy will whisper in our ears, "Just act on your desires and you will be satisfied." But engaging in sexual sin is like trying to quench our thirst by drinking salt water. How have you seen someone you care about (maybe even yourself) begin drinking the lies of lust and ending up wandering deeper and deeper into this world of sin?

In what ways has God designed healthy, biblical, covenantal intimacy as a gift that actually satisfies our desires and fills our needs? Why is it critically important for married Christian couples to make sure their romantic and physical relationship is healthy and thriving?

6. **Read James 1:14–15 and Proverbs 7:22–23.** Lust is a killer! Being hooked by the enticement of this demonic power always leads to death. But this death takes many shapes and forms. Think about the kinds of death that can enter your life if you follow the lure of lust and let it snare you. What might death look like in the following areas?

In your marriage?

In your family?

In your trust with others?

In your creativity?

In your intimacy with God?

In your freedom?

In your peace?

Why is it helpful to reflect honestly and deeply on some of the possible consequences of sin rather than acting as if it is no big deal and you will never get caught?

7. **Read 2 Corinthians 10:3–5, Revelation 12:10–11,** and **Ephesians 6:17.** How is the blood of Jesus (His cross and sacrificial death) the greatest weapon against the demonic work of lust? How should we use this weapon in our day-to-day battles?

How is the Bible, the Word of God, a powerful weapon in our battle against the enticements lust throws our way? How do we use this "sword" in the daily battle?

8. Strongholds can be good or bad. God wants to be our stronghold, our fortress, and our mighty tower. But we can let lustful thoughts and actions become a false stronghold, and we can find ourselves running to these sinful patterns in the misguided belief they will comfort us. How is God our true fortress and stronghold? Why is He the only source of the comfort, hope, and strength we need?

_____

How can lust become a false stronghold that "seems" to fortify us but actually puts us in a prison cell on death row?

_____

We have to replace evil thoughts with good thoughts.

9. **Read Philippians 4:8** and **1 Peter 2:12.** God wants us to break free from the prison of lust and sexual enticements. One of the primary ways to do this is to train our thought lives. Take time as a group to make a list of some of the things we can and should be meditating on as we walk through our days. Use the key words from Philippians 4:8 to get you started on what things we should think about, meditate on, and fill our minds with:

True things

_____

Noble things

_____

Just things

_____

Pure things

_____

Lovely things

_____

Things of good report

_____

Virtuous things

_____

Praiseworthy things

_____

In what ways can we keep these things in our minds even when the world and the enemy throw lustful images and ideas in our faces?

_____

_____

Your destiny depends on which train of thought you board.

10. As Christians who long to honor God and walk in the footsteps of Jesus, it is not enough to meditate on the good; we have to actively fight against the enticements and attacks of the enemy. List a few of the most common sources of lust-producing content in our culture today.

_____

_____

What active steps can we take to ignore, resist, shut off, block out, or run away from these demonic enticements? How can we be praying for each other as we seek to live in holiness and resist the snare of lust?

_____

_____

Closing Prayer

Spend time in your group praying and calling out to God in any of the following ways:

- Thank God that His Word is honest and straightforward about the reality of lust and the consequences of being snared by this powerful spirit.

- Invite God to help you see the severe consequences and cost of walking down the road of lust-filled sin.

- Ask the Holy Spirit to keep your heart and mind fixated on what is good, pure, and praiseworthy.

- Pray for power (for yourself and group members) to resist any and all lustful enticements that come your way.

- Cry out, in the power of the blood of Jesus, for deliverance for anyone in your life (yourself included) who has been snared by this evil and death-filled spirit.

- Pray for discipline to open God's Word every day and learn the truth God reveals in His amazing book.

God always offers deliverance. An escape route is always possible. None of us need to be trapped by sin.

Between-Sessions Personal Study

Reflect further by exploring additional material from Scripture and from Truly Free.

Become a Tactician

Spend time in the coming week studying Proverbs 7 closely.

First, make a list of every **tactic** you see the woman (the spirit of sexual sin and lust) using against the man in this passage:

Next, make a list of the **mistakes** the man (who represents each of us) made when enticed by lust. Where did he go wrong? How did he wander deeper into temptation and finally sin?

Finally, list some of these **same tactics** the enemy is using against you. How are you wandering down the wrong path? What specific steps can you take to repent, change, or run away? What do you need to do to break any patterns of openness to the enticements of lust?

Don't Walk Alone

Most lust-driven sin takes place when we are alone. Our struggles with sexual sin often isolate us, and we begin to avoid the brothers and sisters in Christ who would keep us accountable and call us to repentance. For this reason, we need to make sure we are not walking alone.

If you are a man, get into an accountability group with brothers in the faith. If you are a woman, do the same and find a circle of strong and godly women who will call you out and keep you accountable. Make sure you have one or two friends you can call any time if you are feeling enticed by sinful lures … but particularly lust-driven temptations.

If you have fallen deep into lust-driven sinful patterns, get whatever help you need. Don't walk alone. Bring this into the light. Meet with a pastor. Contact a Christian counselor. Find a wise and older mentor. But do not walk alone any longer.

Jesus set me free—and He can set you free too.

The Blood and the Word

Your two greatest weapons in this battle will always be the **blood of the cross** and the **Word of truth**. When you are struggling, cry out to Jesus. Plead His blood and hold to His name, for there is power in the name and blood of Jesus. Hold to the resurrected Savior and declare that His sacrifice in your place and victory over death broke the power of sin. Speak against any spiritual attack coming against you and declare the victory of Jesus!

Look up the following passages for additional study, reflection, and meditation. Write in your own words what each passage is saying to you.

Exodus 12:1–30

Matthew 26:26–29

Hebrews 9:11–22

1 John 1:7

Revelation 1:5 and 12:11

Also, learn to fight back. The sword of the Spirit is the Word of God (Ephesians 6:17). Open God's Word daily. Read it. Study it. Memorize passages that speak to the power of God over sin. Learn to use this weapon in your daily battle against any enticement the enemy sends your way.

Look up the following passages for additional study, reflection, and meditation. Write in your own words what each passage is saying to you.

Joshua 1:7–9

Psalm 119

2 Timothy 3:16–17

Hebrews 4:12–13

James 1:21–27

Journal

Use the space provided below to write reflections on any of the following questions:

- What are three or four verses I should meditate on and memorize so they are always close to my heart, deep in my mind, and on my tongue?

- What steps have I made and what good measures have I put into place to protect myself from the onslaught of lust-filled content in our world?

- How can I increase my fortification against the flood of lust-producing content in our world?

- What kinds of death have I seen in the lives of people I love because they have fallen into lust-driven patterns and behaviors?

- What are some of the good examples I have seen of people who have stayed pure and resisted these temptations? What can I learn from their lives?

- What is the Holy Spirit saying to me through this session?

Recommended Reading

In preparation for the next session, read chapter ten of *Truly Free*. Use the space below to write any key points or questions you want to bring to the final group meeting.

Session Six

SET FREE

For you were called to freedom.

GALATIANS 5:13 (NASB)

Introduction

We all have times in life when we are living with such anticipation of a moment that when it finally comes, we are simply bursting with excitement. We think about it, dream about it, and long for these moments. Moments such as ...

When we get our first bike.

When we go out on a first date.

When we exchange a first kiss.

When we get to drive our parents' car for the first time.

When we get our first job ... and our first paycheck.

When we stand with our beloved before God, family, and friends and declare, "As long as we both shall live."

There are certain times in life that can be categorized as *the moment we've been waiting for.* All of these get locked away in our hearts because they are significant and life-impacting. But imagine people living in slavery. Every day of their lives they are aware of the fact they are in bondage. They hope and pray for freedom but wonder if it will ever come.

There are people who lived their whole lives in slavery and died that way. But there are those who experienced freedom and felt the cold steel of shackles removed from their wrists and ankles. At that moment of release, these people understood the new life that came when they were truly set free.

Today many people are in spiritual slavery: men and women who love Jesus, but the chains of demonic bondage are locked around their minds, attitudes, and behaviors. They have never experienced the freedom and deliverance they long for. They have not had that life-transforming moment when the power of Jesus broke in, the shackles fell away, and they declared with boundless joy, "This is the moment I have been waiting for!"

If you have been waiting for that moment—longing for it and praying for it—stop right now and pray this prayer:

> *Lord Jesus, I am ready! I know You are greater than the enemy. I know You broke the power of sin, death, hell, and Satan when You shed Your blood on the cross and rose from*

*the dead in glory. Open my heart to learn today. Show me
there is a road to freedom and deliverance, and help me walk
in it today. In Your name, resurrected Jesus, show me where I
am in any form of spiritual bondage, and set me free. Amen!*

Too many people never get delivered
from bondage because they don't realize
in the first place they can be in bondage.

Talk About It

*To get things started for this final session, discuss one of the following
questions:*

- Tell about a time you vividly remember when you found yourself saying or feeling, "This is the moment I have been waiting for!"

- Tell about a time you experienced spiritual freedom from the work,
  presence, or bondage of Satan in your life. What led to this freedom?

All that we value can be under the Lordship of Christ,
never to be stolen away.

Video Teaching Notes

*As you watch the video teaching segment for session six, use the following
outline to record anything that stands out to you. In particular, ask the Holy
Spirit to help you honestly assess where you need to experience freedom and
what steps you need to take to become truly free.*

God wants us to experience both deliverance and discipleship.

There are four keys to being set free. First, we **recognize** we need help. We will never experience freedom if we refuse to admit we are in bondage.

Second, we **repent** to God and others. Repenting means changing our minds about our sins. It involves confession as well—we confess to the Lord and others to bring our sins into the light.

Third, we **renounce** the lies of Satan. All bondage begins with a lie.

Fourth, we **receive** the gifts of the Father. In the story of the lost son told in Luke 15:11–32, the father gave his youngest son a robe, a ring, and sandals. In the spiritual, the robe could represent **righteousness**. To be set free, we must receive God's forgiveness and righteousness.

The ring represents God's **authority** over the enemy. Jesus gave us authority to trample demonic spirits (see Luke 10:19).

_____

_____

_____

_____

The sandals represent **power.** Power is not *something*; it is *Someone.*

_____

_____

_____

_____

When we tell Satan to go, he has to go in Jesus' name. God wants us to be truly free from bondage.

_____

_____

_____

_____

> Repentance, true repentance,
> is crucial for finding freedom.

Bible Study and Group Discussion

Take a few minutes with your group members to discuss what you just watched and explore these concepts in Scripture.

1. In the video, Pastor Morris explained that when he finally understood a Christian can be in spiritual bondage, it brought him hope because it explained how he could be trying so hard to change his behavior but not be able to do it. Why would such a realization bring a person hope? Why is it critically important for Christians to ad-

mit they can be in spiritual bondage? What are some possible consequences if we deny this?

_____

_____

_____

> The main way we can tell if a problem is demonically related is the inability to overcome it on our own.

2. **Read Luke 15:11 – 32.** What are some of the spiritual pigpens Christians find themselves living in today? Why does it take so long for us to realize what we are living in (spiritually) and then want to get out of these situations?

_____

_____

_____

3. When was a time you came to your senses and realized you were living in a spiritual pigpen?

_____

_____

_____

Why was it hard for you to admit your spiritual condition? What finally broke through and allowed you to see your spiritual situation for what it was?

_____

_____

_____

> Did you know it's possible for a son or daughter of the living God to live in a pigpen?

4. **Read Luke 15:1 – 20.** Notice the father in this story does not go and find the younger son and bring him home. What changes happened in the son's thinking and acting that brought him home and set the stage for his freedom and restoration? How does this reflect our part in changing our thinking and actions when it comes to the bondage we face?

_____

_____

_____

5. Confession is not enough — we also need to repent! What is confession? Why is it essential for deliverance from spiritual bondage?

_____

_____

_____

What is repentance? Why is it also essential for deliverance? How do confession and repentance work together for our freedom?

_____

_____

_____

Confession brings forgiveness!
Repentance brings freedom!

6. Our confession is first to God and then to the others we have hurt and wronged while walking in spiritual bondage. Why do you think God wants us to confess to other people? How can this be part of our journey of freedom?

_____

_____

_____

7. **Read Luke 15:25 – 30.** Note that the older brother was also in bondage. He was captured in his own set of lies. What are some of the lies the older brother was telling himself? How did these lead to bondage?

_____

_____

_____

What are some of the lies the enemy and his demonic workers seek to tell God's people today? How do these lies lead to spiritual bondage?

_____

_____

_____

What are some of the lies the enemy is telling you right now … that you are believing? How can your group members pray for you and speak truth to you?

_____

_____

_____

Here's a fact: every bondage begins with a lie.

8. **Read Luke 15:22 – 24.** When the son came home, confessed, repented, and was restored to the Father, he was lavished with gifts. Work as a group to make a list of at least ten gifts our Father in heaven wants to give His children:

- _____   - _____
- _____   - _____
- _____   - _____
- _____   - _____
- _____   - _____

Now, make a list of some of the gifts we start to lose or are not fully enjoying when we are living in bondage:

- _____   - _____
- _____   - _____

- _____   • _____
- _____   • _____
- _____   • _____

9. **Read Isaiah 61:10, Luke 10:19, Ephesians 6:15,** and **Acts 1:8.** There are three gifts God wants to lavish on us as His children. Describe what each can look like in our lives, and talk about how each gift can be used for the glory of God.

Gift #1: Righteousness

What does this gift look like in the life of one who is truly free?

_____

_____

_____

How can this gift be used for the glory of God?

_____

_____

_____

Gift #2: Authority

What does this gift look like in the life of one who is truly free?

_____

_____

_____

How can this gift be used for the glory of God?

_____

_____

_____

Gift #3: Power (to share the gospel)

What does this gift look like in the life of one who is truly free?

_____

_____

_____

How can this gift be used for the glory of God?

_____

_____

_____

10. Ask your group members to pray with you and for you in an area where you are not fully free. Share where you need freedom, the lies you are believing, and what confession and repentance will look like in your life. Invite them to pray, challenge, and check in with you to see how you are doing.

_____

_____

_____

> Repentance is both a one-time act we do at our salvation and an ongoing act we need to do on a regular basis.

Closing Prayer

Spend time in your group praying and calling out to God in any of the following ways. Some of these topics are more personal, so feel free to speak to the Lord alone about them:

- Declare boldly your need for deliverance and freedom from the snares and bondage of the enemy.

- Acknowledge the lies the enemy is speaking to you and declare them as lies.

- Pray the truth of God in response to any lie you have been believing.

- Ask for a heart that is ready to receive every gift God wants to give you and commit to use those gifts for the glory of God.

- Thank the Holy Spirit that He will always live in you as a loved child of God. Ask for the full presence and power of the Spirit in every area of your life.

Recognize you need help.

Personal Study
for the Coming Days

Reflect further by exploring additional material from Scripture and from Truly Free.

Digging Deep

As you walk through the process of freedom, dig deep and be painfully honest with yourself. Complete the following steps:

- Contact anyone from whom you need to **ask forgiveness**. If God places a person on your heart, do all you can to get voice-to-voice with that person and ask him or her to forgive you. You can't control that individual's response, but you can do your part to build a bridge of forgiveness.

- **Confess every sin** the Holy Spirit convicts you of and places on your heart. Don't hold back any of them. If God calls you to confess them to a certain person, do it!

- **Renounce every lie** of the enemy you have been believing. Think through various areas of your life and identify the lies. Then renounce them and speak the truth.

Do you want to be set free? There's a condition.
Repentance is a must.

Renounce the Lie and Tell the Truth

Make a list of lies the devil tries to tell the children of God. Come up with at least ten:

Lies

1. _____
2. _____
3. _____
4. _____
5. _____
6. _____
7. _____
8. _____
9. _____
10. _____

Next, find one or two passages in the Bible that speak the truth into each topic and refute the enemy's lie. Use this as a resource any time you hear the enemy whisper one of these lies into your ear.

God's Truth

1. _____
2. _____
3. _____
4. _____
5. _____
6. _____
7. _____
8. _____
9. _____
10. _____

For us to get free, we must renounce the lies of Satan.
We do that by immersing our minds in God's Word.

Declare It!

Sometimes it is helpful to have a prayer or declaration to lift up when we are facing spiritual battles and seeking deliverance. Here is a short affirmation taken from a number of passages in the Bible. Use this as a way to speak the truth when the enemy is attacking you with lies:

I am born again through Jesus Christ, the Word of God, and kept by the power of God.
I am sealed by the Holy Spirit of promise.
I have authority over all the power of the enemy in the name of Jesus.
Nothing shall by any means harm me.
I am more than a conqueror through Christ, who loves me.
Jesus always causes me to triumph in His name.
Greater is He that is in me than he that is in the world!

Journal

Use the space provided below to write reflections on any of the following questions:

- What declaration can I make to state that, although the Holy Spirit lives in me through faith in Jesus, I can be enticed into spiritual bondage?

- What are some of the things I still need to confess and repent of?

- What are some recurring lies the enemy seeks to tell me?

- What are some of the great gifts of God I need to acknowledge, thank Him for, and use more intentionally for His glory?

- What is the Holy Spirit saying to me through this session?

_____

Recommended Reading

For ongoing study and personal growth in freedom, consider reading chapters five, six, eight, nine, and the appendices in _Truly Free._

_____

SMALL GROUP
LEADER HELPS

To ensure a successful small group experience, read the following information before beginning.

Group Preparation

Whether your small group has been meeting together for years or is gathering for the first time, be sure to designate a consistent time and place to work through the six sessions. Once you establish the when and where of your times together, select a facilitator who will keep discussions on track and an eye on the clock. If you choose to rotate this responsibility, assign the six sessions to their respective facilitators up front so that group members can prepare their thoughts and questions prior to the session they are responsible for leading. Follow the same assignment procedure should your group want to serve any snacks/beverages.

A Note to Facilitators

As facilitator, you are responsible for honoring the agreed-upon timeframe of each meeting, for prompting helpful discussion among your group, and for keeping the dialogue equitable by drawing out quieter members and helping more talkative members to remember that others' insights are valued in your group.

You might find it helpful to preview each session's video teaching segment (they range from 20–22 minutes) and then scan the discussion questions and Bible passages that pertain to it, highlighting various questions that you want to be sure to cover during your group's meeting. Ask God in advance of your time together to guide your group's discussion, and then be sensitive to the direction He wishes to lead.

Urge participants to bring their study guide, pen, and a Bible to every gathering. Encourage them to consider buying a copy of the book *Truly Free* by Robert Morris to supplement this study.

Session Format

Each session of the study guide includes the following group components:

- **"Introduction"** — an entrée to the session's topic, which may be read by a volunteer or summarized by the facilitator

- **"Talk About It"** — icebreaker questions that relate to the session topic and invite input from every group member (select one, or use both options if time permits)

- **"Video Teaching Notes"** — an outline of the session's video teaching segment for group members to follow along and take notes if they wish

- **"Bible Study and Group Discussion"** — video-related and Bible exploration questions that reinforce the session content and elicit personal input from every group member

- **"Closing Prayer"** — several prayer cues to guide group members in closing prayer

Additionally, in each session you will find a **"Between-Sessions Personal Study"** section (**"Personal Study for the Coming Days"** for session six) that includes more Bible exploration, suggestions for personal actions, a journaling opportunity, and recommended reading from the *Truly Free* book.

WHAT'S KEEPING YOU FROM BEING TRULY FREE?

{ ROBERT MORRIS HAS A REMARKABLE WAY OF KNOWING WHERE I LIVE AND HELPING ME MOVE FORWARD. I LOVE HIM AND HIS TEACHING.
—MAX LUCADO }

In 2004, Pastor Robert Morris transformed the act of giving in his bestseller *The Blessed Life*, and now he does the same for spiritual freedom in his new book, *Truly Free*.

If you've ever wondered, *Why do I keep repeating the same mistakes over and over again? Why can't I change?* Take heart—there is a way out! With relevant scriptures, prayers, and questions for contemplation or group discussion, this book explains how you can find a lasting freedom and live truly free.

Best-Selling Author of *The Blessed Life* and *The God I Never Knew*

ROBERT MORRIS

Breaking the Snares That So Easily Entangle

TRULY FREE

THOMAS NELSON
®
Since 1798

AVAILABLE WHEREVER BOOKS AND EBOOKS ARE SOLD!

9780718011103-A